AI PROFIT PLAYBOOK FOR EVERYDAY ENTREPRENEURS

PRACTICAL SYSTEMS TO TURN SMART TOOLS INTO DAILY INCOME

DESHAWN PRICE

HERITAGE HOUSE
PUBLISHING

This book is dedicated to the everyday entrepreneur — the builder who works quietly before sunrise, the thinker who refuses to settle for limitation, and the dreamer who believes that opportunity belongs not only to the powerful but to the persistent. To those who are learning new tools while juggling real responsibilities, who are building something meaningful in the margins of busy lives, and who dare to believe that intelligent leverage can change the trajectory of their future — this playbook is for you.

It is dedicated to the operators who choose discipline over distraction, progress over perfection, and execution over endless planning. To the creators who understand that technology is not the destination but the amplifier of vision, courage, and service. You are proof that innovation does not belong exclusively to giant corporations or elite circles; it belongs to anyone willing to learn, adapt, and act consistently.

I also dedicate this work to the mentors, pioneers, and innovators whose bold thinking reshaped how the world views possibility — those who proved that imagination combined with relentless execution can redefine entire industries. Their influence reminds us that the future is built by people who think differently and move decisively.

Most of all, this dedication belongs to those who are building not just income, but impact — families seeking stability, creators pursuing freedom, and entrepreneurs determined to turn ideas into lasting value. May this book serve as a practical companion, a steady guide, and a reminder that your daily decisions matter more than any single breakthrough moment.

Your tools are powerful. Your opportunity is real. Your next chapter begins now.

“In a world powered by artificial intelligence, the true advantage is still human intention.”

FOREWORD

We are living in a moment that previous generations would have described as impossible.

For centuries, economic power has followed infrastructure. The companies with the most capital, the largest teams, and the widest distribution networks controlled opportunity. The individual entrepreneur, no matter how gifted, faced structural limitations. Time was finite. Talent was expensive. Scale required permission.

Artificial intelligence has disrupted that model.

For the first time in modern history, an everyday entrepreneur with a laptop, focus, and discipline can operate with capabilities that once required entire departments. Research that took weeks can now be done in minutes. Content that required teams can be structured in hours. Systems that demanded specialists can be built and optimized by a single determined operator.

But here is the truth this book makes clear: AI does not create profit. Operators do.

Technology amplifies direction. If direction is scattered, results will be scattered. If direction is strategic, results compound. The entrepreneurs who win in this new era will not be the ones who chase every new feature. They will be the ones who build intelligent systems around timeless principles — clarity, value creation, disciplined execution, and measurable improvement.

This playbook does not treat AI as magic. It treats it as leverage.

Inside these pages, you will find practical systems designed for real people with real constraints. You will learn how to structure workflows, design offers, build funnels, create digital assets, and automate intelligently without losing your voice or integrity. You will see how to move from scattered experimentation to structured execution, from side income to sustainable enterprise.

Most importantly, you will see that the advantage does not belong to corporations alone. It belongs to individuals willing to think like operators.

The opportunity is real. The tools are accessible. The path is practical.

What happens next depends on whether you build.

INTRODUCTION

We are standing at the edge of a new economic era — one where intelligence is no longer limited to large companies, specialized teams, or massive budgets. Artificial intelligence has quietly shifted the balance of power, placing extraordinary leverage into the hands of everyday entrepreneurs. What once required departments, consultants, and years of trial and error can now be executed with clarity and speed by individuals willing to learn and act. This shift is not theoretical. It is practical, immediate, and already reshaping how income is created around the world.

Yet with all this opportunity comes a new challenge. Many people see AI as overwhelming, confusing, or filled with endless distractions. New tools appear daily, promises are exaggerated, and entrepreneurs often find themselves busy without becoming profitable. The problem is not access to technology — it is the lack of a clear operating system for using it effectively. Without structure, AI becomes noise. With structure, it becomes leverage.

This book was written to provide that structure.

AI Profit Playbook for Everyday Entrepreneurs is not

about hype, shortcuts, or unrealistic promises. It is a practical guide designed to help you think like an operator — someone who builds systems that produce consistent results. The goal is simple: turn smart tools into daily income through clarity, focus, and repeatable processes. You do not need to be a programmer, a tech expert, or a venture-backed founder. You need a willingness to learn, experiment, and execute with discipline.

Inside these pages, you will discover how to choose profitable directions, create offers that solve real problems, build marketing systems that attract buyers, automate intelligently without losing authenticity, and scale from side income into sustainable business. Each chapter is designed to move you from understanding to implementation, from ideas to action.

The truth is this: AI is not the opportunity. You are.

The tools are only multipliers. They amplify whatever strategy, effort, and vision you bring to them. If you build wisely, they will expand your reach, your efficiency, and your impact. If you drift without direction, they will only magnify confusion.

This book is your invitation to build with intention.

The future will belong to those who combine human creativity with intelligent systems. The entrepreneurs who win will not necessarily be the smartest or the most technical — they will be the most consistent, the most focused, and the most willing to execute.

Your playbook starts now.

PREFACE

This book was born out of a simple observation: the rules of entrepreneurship have changed faster than most people realize.

For years, building a profitable business required significant capital, specialized knowledge, and access to resources that were often out of reach for everyday individuals. Many talented entrepreneurs had ideas but lacked leverage. They worked hard, yet progress felt slow because effort alone could not compete with scale.

Then artificial intelligence arrived — not as a distant concept, but as a practical tool available to anyone willing to learn.

What fascinated me most was not the technology itself, but what it represented. For the first time, ordinary entrepreneurs could operate with extraordinary capability. One person could research faster, create faster, market smarter, and execute with a level of efficiency that once belonged only to large organizations. The barrier between vision and execution began to shrink.

Yet I also noticed something else.

Many people were overwhelmed. They were experimenting endlessly but not building systems. They were using tools without direction. They were busy — but not profitable. The missing piece was not access to AI; it was a practical framework for turning intelligent tools into consistent income.

This book was written to close that gap.

The pages that follow are not meant to impress with technical complexity. They are designed to provide clarity. The focus is on practical systems — workflows, strategies, and decision-making frameworks that help everyday entrepreneurs move from scattered effort to structured execution. Every chapter is built around one core belief: technology should simplify business, not complicate it.

As you read, you will notice a recurring theme. AI is powerful, but it is not the hero of this story. The entrepreneur is. Tools amplify intention. They multiply discipline. They accelerate direction. But they cannot replace vision, character, or consistent action.

My hope is that this book becomes more than information. I hope it becomes a working guide you return to repeatedly — a playbook you apply, refine, and grow with as your business evolves. Whether you are starting with a side income idea or scaling toward something larger, the principles here are designed to help you build something sustainable.

The opportunity is real. The tools are available. The timing could not be better.

Now the only question is what you will build with them.

1

AI PROFIT PLAYBOOK FOR EVERYDAY ENTREPRENEURS - PRACTICAL SYSTEMS TO TURN SMART TOOLS INTO DAILY INCOME

We are living through one of the greatest economic shifts in modern history. Artificial intelligence is no longer reserved for tech giants, engineers, or billion-dollar startups. It has quietly moved into the hands of everyday entrepreneurs — people with vision, creativity, and the willingness to act. The rules of business are changing, and those who understand how to harness intelligent tools today will shape the income opportunities of tomorrow.

This book is not about theory, hype, or futuristic speculation. It is about practical systems. It is about turning tools into leverage, leverage into value, and value into daily income streams that can grow steadily over time. AI does not replace entrepreneurs — it multiplies them. It removes friction, accelerates execution, and gives small operators capabilities that once required entire teams.

The truth is simple: most people will use AI for entertainment or convenience. A smaller group will use it for efficiency. But a rare group — the builders, the operators, the everyday entrepreneurs — will use AI as a profit engine.

This playbook is written for that group. It is designed for the person who may not have a large budget, a technical background, or a massive audience, but who understands the power of consistent action and intelligent systems.

Inside these pages, you will discover frameworks that simplify decision-making, strategies that create scalable income opportunities, and workflows that allow you to compete in a rapidly evolving digital economy. The goal is not complexity; it is clarity. The goal is not chasing trends; it is building sustainable momentum.

AI is not the opportunity. You are. This book simply hands you the playbook to turn smart tools into real results — one system, one decision, and one profitable action at a time.

2

THE AI PROFIT SHIFT

The world has quietly crossed a line that many people still fail to see clearly. Artificial intelligence has moved from laboratories and enterprise systems into the hands of everyday entrepreneurs who once lacked scale, capital, and technical advantage. For decades, leverage belonged to those with teams, infrastructure, and financial dominance, but AI has redistributed that power in ways that are both disruptive and deeply democratizing. The solo creator, the small business owner, and the independent operator now possess tools capable of multiplying output without multiplying overhead. This is not a temporary trend or a passing wave of technology excitement; it is a structural shift in how value is created and delivered. The entrepreneur who learns to think in systems rather than tasks suddenly finds their time stretching farther than ever before. What once required departments can now be executed by one focused individual with intelligent assistance. The greatest shift is not technological but psychological, because AI changes how people approach problems and opportunities. Those who recognize this moment early will build momentum while others remain trapped in outdated business models. The AI profit shift begins the moment an entrepreneur realizes that leverage is no longer reserved for the powerful but available to the prepared.

Historically, the advantage of large businesses came from their ability to hire specialists, automate processes, and dominate attention through sheer scale. Small operators were forced to choose between quality and speed, often sacrificing one to maintain the other. AI collapses that old tradeoff by enabling rapid production without sacrificing strategic thinking or creative direction. A single entrepreneur can now produce marketing campaigns, analyze customer behavior, generate professional content, and refine offers at a pace that once required full-time staff. This shift creates a new economic reality where agility outweighs size and experimentation outruns bureaucracy. Large companies still possess resources, but they move slowly under layers of approval and process. Everyday entrepreneurs, however, can pivot instantly, test ideas quickly, and adapt messaging in real time using AI-driven insights. The power gap narrows when intelligence becomes accessible rather than exclusive. Instead of competing on size, small operators compete on speed, relevance, and precision. In this new landscape, the entrepreneur who learns fast wins faster than the company that moves cautiously.

The greatest misconception surrounding AI is that it replaces human effort or creativity, when in reality it amplifies intentional direction. Tools do not create profit by themselves; entrepreneurs create profit through decisions, positioning, and execution. AI simply removes friction between idea and implementation, allowing concepts to reach the marketplace with unprecedented speed. When used correctly, it acts as a multiplier that enhances clarity, refines messaging, and accelerates iteration cycles. The entrepreneur remains the architect, while AI becomes the engine that carries the blueprint forward. This distinction matters because those who rely blindly on tools produce generic results that quickly disappear into noise. Those who apply vision, strategy, and market understanding generate outcomes that stand out and attract attention. The AI profit shift rewards operators who think critically rather than passively. Success comes from combining human judgment with machine efficiency in a balanced way. The future belongs not to artificial intelligence alone, but to augmented entrepreneurs who understand how to direct it wisely.

Everyday entrepreneurs possess hidden advantages that become amplified in an AI-driven economy. They are close to their customers, close to their problems, and close to the emotional realities that drive purchasing decisions. Unlike large corporations that rely on slow market research cycles, small operators can listen, respond, and adjust instantly. AI enhances this closeness by helping entrepreneurs analyze patterns, generate ideas, and test messaging rapidly without large budgets. This creates a powerful feedback loop where learning happens faster and improvements happen continuously. Small businesses no longer need perfect plans before launching; they need adaptive systems that evolve with data and real-world response. AI enables experimentation without catastrophic risk because iteration costs become dramatically lower. The entrepreneur who embraces fast testing gains insight that competitors cannot replicate quickly. Speed becomes a strategic weapon rather than a reckless gamble. In this environment, small operators stop competing for scraps and begin shaping markets of their own.

One of the most profound changes brought by AI is the collapse of traditional barriers to entry. Skills that once required years of training can now be supported by intelligent systems that guide execution and reduce technical complexity. Entrepreneurs can create products, design branding, write compelling copy, and build automated workflows without hiring expensive specialists. This does not eliminate expertise, but it does make expertise accessible to those willing to learn and apply frameworks. The result is a surge of opportunity for people who previously felt locked out of digital business models. Everyday entrepreneurs are no longer spectators watching innovation from the sidelines. They are participants capable of launching offers quickly and refining them through data-driven feedback. AI lowers the cost of mistakes while increasing the speed of learning. The competitive advantage shifts toward those willing to experiment and iterate consistently. Opportunity expands for those who choose action over hesitation.

Attention has become the most valuable currency in the modern economy, and AI changes how attention is earned and maintained. Large companies once dominated visibility through advertising budgets that smaller competitors could never match. Today, intelligent tools allow entrepreneurs to create high-quality content, optimize messaging, and publish consistently across platforms without burnout. Consistency builds trust, and trust converts attention into revenue over time. AI makes consistency sustainable by reducing the effort required to produce meaningful output. Entrepreneurs who previously struggled to maintain marketing momentum now gain a steady rhythm of creation and distribution. This steady presence creates authority, and authority creates opportunity. The AI profit shift rewards those who show up daily with value-driven content and clear positioning. Visibility becomes less about spending money and more about executing smart systems. The entrepreneur who learns to harness AI for attention will never feel invisible again.

Competing with larger businesses no longer means imitating their strategies or trying to outspend them. Instead, it means building lean systems that outperform heavy structures through efficiency and adaptability. AI allows small operators to operate with precision, identifying what works and eliminating what does not without wasting resources. Decision-making becomes faster because data and insights are accessible instantly. Entrepreneurs can refine offers, improve customer experiences, and adjust pricing with confidence rather than guesswork. Large organizations often struggle to change direction quickly because their scale creates inertia. Smaller businesses thrive because they can shift course without disruption. AI strengthens this agility by providing clarity that guides action. The result is a business model designed for momentum rather than maintenance. Everyday entrepreneurs who embrace this approach stop feeling small and start thinking strategically powerful.

The emotional shift behind AI adoption is just as important as the technical shift. Many entrepreneurs carry years of frustration from trying to do everything alone while competing against overwhelming odds. AI introduces a new feeling: capability. Tasks that once felt exhausting become manageable, and ideas that once felt impossible become executable. This psychological momentum creates confidence, and confidence fuels consistent action. Entrepreneurs begin to see themselves not as underdogs but as operators equipped with modern leverage. When mindset changes, behavior changes, and when behavior changes, results follow naturally. AI becomes more than a tool; it becomes a catalyst for belief in what is possible. The profit shift begins internally before it manifests externally. Those who adopt a growth-oriented perspective will experience acceleration that feels almost exponential.

The long-term winners in the AI era will not be those who chase every new tool or trend. They will be the entrepreneurs who build repeatable systems that generate predictable outcomes over time. AI should simplify operations rather than complicate them, turning chaos into clarity and effort into momentum. Everyday entrepreneurs thrive when they focus on sustainable processes that can be repeated daily without burnout. Profit grows when systems remove decision fatigue and allow consistent execution. This is where small operators gain a permanent advantage over larger competitors who rely on rigid structures. AI enables flexibility while maintaining structure, creating a balance that supports long-term growth. The entrepreneur who masters systems becomes resilient against market shifts and technological change. Stability emerges from disciplined application rather than constant reinvention. The AI profit shift ultimately rewards consistency more than brilliance.

We stand at the beginning of an era where intelligence itself becomes a resource accessible to anyone willing to use it wisely. The entrepreneur who embraces AI today is not simply adopting a new tool but stepping into a new operating model for business and income creation. The playing field is no longer defined by size, funding, or traditional gatekeepers but by speed of learning and clarity of execution. Everyday entrepreneurs have been handed a rare opportunity to compete at levels previously unimaginable. The question is no longer whether AI will change business but who will choose to leverage it fully. Those who wait for certainty will watch others build momentum ahead of them. Those who act with intentional strategy will discover that daily income is not built through luck but through intelligent systems repeated consistently. The AI profit shift is already happening, and the only decision left is whether to observe it or participate in it. The playbook begins here, with a mindset that sees leverage where others still see limitation.

3

THE EVERYDAY ENTREPRENEUR ADVANTAGE

The everyday entrepreneur stands at a rare intersection of opportunity where technology meets personal initiative, and that intersection creates momentum that larger organizations often struggle to replicate. Speed has always been a defining advantage of small operators, but artificial intelligence transforms that speed into a powerful economic weapon. While corporations spend months in meetings, reviews, and approval cycles, individuals can move from idea to execution in a single day. AI compresses research, content creation, planning, and delivery into workflows that once required teams and budgets. This means that the person with a clear idea and decisive action can reach the market before a larger competitor finishes planning. The entrepreneur's advantage is not just moving quickly but learning quickly, adjusting quickly, and improving quickly. Every experiment becomes data, and every result becomes insight that fuels the next decision. AI amplifies this loop by making iteration almost effortless compared to traditional methods. The modern entrepreneur who understands this dynamic realizes that velocity itself becomes a competitive moat. In an AI-driven economy, speed is no longer reckless movement but disciplined execution at a pace others cannot match.

Flexibility is the second pillar of the everyday entrepreneur's advantage, and AI multiplies it beyond what previous generations imagined possible. Large organizations often rely on rigid structures designed for stability rather than adaptation, which makes change expensive and slow. Individual entrepreneurs, however, can shift direction instantly when they see new opportunities or changing market signals. AI helps them analyze trends, test messaging, and adapt offers without rebuilding entire systems. A single change in strategy can be implemented across marketing, product creation, and customer communication within hours. This responsiveness allows small operators to meet customers where they are rather than forcing customers into predetermined models. Flexibility also reduces risk because entrepreneurs are not locked into long-term commitments that drain resources. AI-powered workflows make experimentation inexpensive, turning curiosity into measurable progress. The ability to pivot quickly creates resilience during uncertain markets and emerging trends. In a world that changes daily, the flexible entrepreneur becomes the one who thrives while slower competitors struggle to keep up.

Creativity has always separated exceptional entrepreneurs from average ones, but AI changes how creativity is expressed and scaled. Instead of staring at a blank page or struggling to organize ideas, entrepreneurs can now collaborate with intelligent systems that spark concepts and accelerate execution. Creativity becomes less about waiting for inspiration and more about directing intelligent tools toward meaningful outcomes. The entrepreneur provides vision, tone, and purpose while AI handles the heavy lifting of expansion and refinement. This partnership allows individuals to produce at levels once reserved for entire creative departments. More importantly, it frees mental energy to focus on strategy, storytelling, and emotional connection with the audience. Creativity paired with speed and flexibility becomes a multiplier that large organizations find difficult to imitate. The entrepreneur who learns to use AI creatively gains the ability to test multiple ideas rapidly and refine the best ones quickly. Innovation stops being occasional and becomes part of daily workflow. The result is a continuous stream of fresh offers and messaging that keeps the business alive and relevant.

Traditional companies often assume their size guarantees dominance, yet size can become a liability when technology shifts rapidly. Bureaucracy slows experimentation, and risk management often suppresses innovation before it reaches the market. Everyday entrepreneurs operate differently because they are closer to both their customers and their decisions. AI gives them access to insights that previously required expensive analytics teams, allowing them to make smarter choices without delay. This means individuals can identify profitable opportunities before larger competitors recognize the trend. Small operators are not burdened by legacy systems or outdated processes that resist change. Instead, they build lean operations designed around efficiency and adaptation. AI reinforces this lean structure by automating repetitive tasks and freeing time for strategic thinking. The entrepreneur becomes a decision-maker rather than a task manager. In this way, AI does not just level the playing field; it tilts it toward those who move decisively.

Monetization speed is one of the clearest ways AI

empowers everyday entrepreneurs to outperform larger businesses. Corporations often require extensive validation before launching new products or services, which delays revenue generation. Entrepreneurs can test offers quickly, gather feedback, and refine pricing in real time. AI helps create prototypes, marketing materials, and customer messaging within hours rather than weeks. This rapid cycle allows individuals to start earning while still improving the product. Instead of waiting for perfection, they launch early and optimize continuously. Revenue becomes part of the development process rather than the final step. AI makes this approach sustainable by reducing the workload associated with testing and iteration. The entrepreneur who monetizes quickly gains cash flow that funds future growth. Speed to revenue becomes a defining advantage that larger companies rarely match.

Another powerful advantage lies in the ability of everyday entrepreneurs to personalize their work at scale. Large companies often struggle to sound human because their messaging passes through layers of approval and branding guidelines. Individuals, however, can maintain authentic voices that resonate deeply with audiences. AI assists by helping entrepreneurs tailor messages to specific customer needs without losing consistency. Personalized content, targeted offers, and adaptive communication create stronger relationships with buyers. Customers increasingly value authenticity over corporate polish, and small operators naturally deliver that authenticity. AI simply amplifies their ability to maintain it while scaling output. This combination of personal connection and efficient production creates a powerful competitive edge. Entrepreneurs can build loyal communities rather than just customer lists. Loyalty translates into repeat revenue and organic growth that large companies spend millions trying to achieve.

Time has always been the greatest limitation for entrepreneurs, but AI changes how time is experienced and used. Tasks that once consumed entire days can now be completed in minutes, creating space for higher-level thinking. Entrepreneurs gain the freedom to focus on strategy, partnerships, and innovation instead of repetitive work. This shift transforms productivity from hustle-driven exhaustion into intentional leverage. AI becomes an extension of the entrepreneur's capabilities, allowing more output without sacrificing energy. The everyday operator can now compete with teams by intelligently delegating to tools rather than employees. This does not eliminate hard work but ensures that effort produces greater results. Time saved becomes opportunity gained, and opportunity compounds over months and years. Entrepreneurs who use AI wisely find themselves accomplishing more while feeling less overwhelmed. The true advantage is not working harder but working smarter with consistent leverage.

The learning curve for entrepreneurship has historically been steep, often discouraging people from pursuing their ideas. AI reduces this barrier by providing guidance, suggestions, and frameworks that accelerate skill development. Entrepreneurs can learn marketing, sales, writing, and strategy through active experimentation supported by intelligent systems. This creates a feedback-rich environment where learning happens through doing rather than waiting for mastery. Traditional companies rely on formal training and long onboarding processes that slow progress. Individuals can educate themselves rapidly while simultaneously building real businesses. AI acts as a mentor that provides immediate support without judgment or delay.

The result is faster growth both personally and professionally. Entrepreneurs who embrace continuous learning gain confidence to explore new opportunities. Knowledge becomes accessible, and accessibility fuels action.

Risk management looks different for everyday entrepreneurs operating in an AI-powered world. Large organizations often avoid risk because mistakes carry enormous financial consequences. Individuals, however, can take calculated risks because AI lowers the cost of experimentation. Testing new ideas becomes inexpensive, and failures provide valuable insights rather than catastrophic losses. Entrepreneurs can run multiple small experiments simultaneously, increasing the chances of finding profitable outcomes. AI helps analyze results quickly, ensuring that lessons are captured and applied immediately. This approach creates a portfolio mindset where small bets lead to big discoveries. The entrepreneur who embraces intelligent experimentation builds resilience and adaptability. Risk transforms from something to fear into something to manage strategically. Over time, this mindset creates consistent innovation and steady growth.

Ultimately, the everyday entrepreneur advantage is about mindset as much as technology. AI is a tool, but the willingness to move quickly, adapt freely, and create boldly defines success. Individuals who see themselves as operators rather than observers unlock the true potential of intelligent systems. They understand that small size is not a weakness but a strategic advantage in a rapidly changing world. Speed allows them to lead trends instead of chasing them. Flexibility allows them to survive uncertainty while others hesitate. Creativity allows them to build unique value that cannot be copied easily. AI amplifies all three traits, turning ordinary entrepreneurs into highly capable competitors. The future belongs to those who act with clarity and consistency rather than waiting for perfect conditions. The everyday entrepreneur who embraces this advantage will discover that the gap between small and large has never been narrower, and opportunity has never been greater.

4

CHOOSING A PROFITABLE AI INCOME PATH

Opportunity without direction quickly becomes distraction, and nowhere is that more evident than in the rapidly expanding world of artificial intelligence. Every week new tools emerge, new promises circulate, and new income claims flood the digital marketplace. The everyday entrepreneur who chases every possibility soon finds energy scattered and results diluted. Choosing a profitable AI income path begins with clarity rather than curiosity. It requires stepping back from the noise and asking a disciplined question about where real value can be created. AI is powerful, but power without focus produces fragmentation instead of momentum. The entrepreneurs who build daily income do not pursue every trend; they pursue one strategic lane with consistency. They treat AI as infrastructure supporting a defined direction rather than entertainment that fills idle time. The moment focus replaces fascination, productivity rises sharply. A profitable path starts when AI becomes a tool serving a mission rather than a novelty consuming attention.

The first decision in choosing a profitable path is identifying a niche that aligns with both market demand and personal capability. A niche is not merely a topic but a concentrated problem experienced by a specific group of people. Broad ambition leads to generic messaging, while defined focus creates resonance and clarity. AI makes research faster, but it cannot replace thoughtful positioning. Entrepreneurs must examine where pain points exist, where money is already flowing, and where they can contribute meaningful solutions. The right niche sits at the intersection of demand, accessibility, and personal interest. AI can assist in analyzing trends, competitors, and customer language to uncover profitable pockets of opportunity. However, selection requires judgment and strategic thinking beyond raw data. The most successful entrepreneurs commit to serving a defined audience instead of chasing universal appeal. Precision in niche selection transforms AI from a general tool into a targeted revenue engine.

Once a niche is identified, the next step is crafting an offer that translates value into measurable results. Many entrepreneurs confuse activity with value, producing content or services without clear outcomes. A profitable offer solves a defined problem in a way that feels specific and actionable. AI accelerates creation, but clarity of outcome determines conversion. Customers pay for transformation, not for tools or features. The entrepreneur must articulate what changes for the buyer after engaging with the product or service. AI can help refine messaging and structure delivery, but the core promise must be deliberate and compelling. A well-defined offer creates confidence in the marketplace and eliminates confusion during sales conversations. When the offer is precise, marketing becomes simpler and more effective. Revenue begins to flow when value is packaged in a way that buyers immediately understand.

Audience identification is equally critical because even the strongest offer fails when presented to the wrong people. AI enables entrepreneurs to study audience behavior, preferences, and language patterns with remarkable speed. However, selecting the right audience requires more than demographic data. It involves understanding emotional drivers, aspirations, and frustrations that influence purchasing decisions. The entrepreneur who knows their audience deeply can create messaging that feels personal and timely. AI assists by generating variations of communication tailored to specific segments. This level of personalization was once reserved for large marketing departments. Today, individuals can craft targeted campaigns that speak directly to defined groups. When audience alignment is achieved, marketing feels like service rather than persuasion. The right audience amplifies every effort because resonance replaces resistance.

A major mistake entrepreneurs make is allowing AI to dictate direction instead of using it to enhance strategy. The availability of tools can create the illusion that every capability must be monetized simultaneously. In reality, sustainable income comes from building depth before breadth. Choosing one primary path allows systems to mature and reputation to grow. AI should streamline execution within a chosen model rather than pull attention toward unrelated experiments. Focus compounds results because each action reinforces previous efforts. Distraction, on the other hand, resets progress and drains momentum. Entrepreneurs who discipline themselves to pursue one profitable avenue discover that growth accelerates naturally. AI becomes an accelerator rather than a detour. Direction precedes scale, and clarity precedes automation.

Validation plays a crucial role in confirming that a chosen path holds real potential. AI makes market testing faster and less expensive than ever before. Entrepreneurs can launch small-scale offers, gather feedback, and measure response without heavy investment. This testing phase transforms assumptions into evidence. Instead of guessing what customers want, operators can observe actual behavior and adjust accordingly. Validation reduces risk while increasing confidence in long-term strategy. AI assists in analyzing feedback and identifying patterns that guide refinement. Small wins during validation build psychological momentum that encourages continued execution. Entrepreneurs who validate early avoid costly missteps later. Profitability emerges when ideas are tested before they are expanded.

Scalability must also be considered when selecting an AI income path. Some opportunities generate short-term revenue but require constant manual effort. Others allow automation and repetition that produce compounding returns. AI excels at supporting scalable models such as digital products, subscription services, and automated marketing systems. The entrepreneur should evaluate whether the chosen niche and offer can grow without proportional increases in workload. Scalability transforms daily income into sustained momentum over time. AI reduces operational friction, making scaling more achievable for individuals. A well-chosen path allows incremental improvements to produce exponential impact. Entrepreneurs who think long term design systems that expand gracefully. Sustainable growth begins with strategic selection rather than reactive experimentation.

Differentiation becomes essential once a path is chosen because competition inevitably increases in profitable markets. AI can generate similar outputs for many users, which means uniqueness must come from positioning and perspective. Entrepreneurs must define what makes their approach distinct within the chosen niche. This differentiation might involve storytelling, specialized frameworks, or unique delivery methods. AI supports execution, but originality remains a human responsibility. Customers are drawn to voices that feel authentic and purposeful. When differentiation is clear, marketing becomes memorable rather than interchangeable. The entrepreneur who defines a unique angle builds defensibility against copycat competitors. AI amplifies distinctive branding when guided intentionally. Standing out requires deliberate strategy rather than accidental variation.

Commitment separates those who dabble from those who build lasting income streams. Once a profitable AI path is selected, consistency becomes the primary driver of results. AI reduces friction, but persistence sustains progress. Entrepreneurs must allocate time, refine processes, and measure performance continuously. The temptation to abandon a path prematurely can sabotage momentum. Growth often appears gradual before it accelerates dramatically. AI supports consistency by automating repetitive tasks and preserving quality across output. This stability creates trust among customers and strengthens brand identity. Entrepreneurs who remain disciplined through early phases position themselves for breakthrough moments. Long-term success emerges from repeated focused effort rather than scattered bursts of activity.

Choosing a profitable AI income path ultimately requires courage to ignore distractions and pursue clarity.

The digital landscape will continue evolving, offering endless possibilities that compete for attention. Entrepreneurs who thrive are those who evaluate options strategically and commit deliberately. AI becomes transformative only when anchored to defined purpose and structured execution. The right niche channels energy, the right offer converts value into revenue, and the right audience multiplies impact. Together, these elements create a stable foundation for daily income generation. The entrepreneur who masters this selection process builds confidence in their direction. Instead of reacting to trends, they operate with intentional focus and measurable progress. AI ceases to be overwhelming and becomes empowering. Profit follows when smart tools are aligned with smart decisions, and discipline turns opportunity into sustained income.

5

BUILDING YOUR AI PRODUCTIVITY ENGINE

Productivity is no longer defined by how many hours you work but by how intelligently those hours are structured. The everyday entrepreneur who embraces artificial intelligence gains access to a new operating model that transforms effort into leverage. Building an AI productivity engine begins with a shift in thinking from isolated tasks to interconnected workflows. Instead of reacting to daily demands, the entrepreneur designs a system that anticipates them. AI becomes the infrastructure supporting ideation, execution, refinement, and distribution in one seamless loop. This engine is not chaotic automation but deliberate architecture built around clear outcomes. Each workflow connects to the next, ensuring that momentum compounds rather than resets each day. The goal is multiplication, not mere completion. When properly structured, the AI productivity engine reduces cognitive overload and decision fatigue. It converts scattered activity into synchronized progress that builds daily income with consistency and clarity.

The foundation of the productivity engine is clarity of objectives because tools without direction create noise. Entrepreneurs must define what output truly matters before introducing automation. Revenue-generating activities take priority over peripheral tasks that drain attention. AI excels when it is assigned specific, measurable objectives rather than vague instructions. Clear goals allow workflows to be engineered around outcomes instead of busywork. This clarity ensures that every automated process serves a strategic purpose. The entrepreneur determines the destination, and AI accelerates the journey. Without defined priorities, productivity tools become distractions disguised as efficiency. With precision, they become amplifiers of meaningful progress. The engine begins with intention and expands through disciplined execution.

Daily workflows must be designed for repeatability because consistency builds predictable income. The entrepreneur identifies recurring tasks such as research, content creation, marketing outreach, and customer engagement. Each task becomes a structured sequence supported by AI assistance. Research can be streamlined through intelligent summarization and trend analysis. Content can be drafted, refined, and optimized within hours rather than days. Marketing messages can be adapted for multiple platforms without rewriting from scratch. Customer responses can be organized and analyzed to uncover patterns for improvement. By mapping these activities into repeatable cycles, entrepreneurs eliminate unnecessary friction. The engine becomes a rhythm rather than a scramble. Repeatable systems transform creativity from sporadic inspiration into dependable output.

Automation plays a central role in reducing effort

while maintaining quality. Many entrepreneurs exhaust themselves by manually performing tasks that AI can handle efficiently. Building the productivity engine requires identifying which actions can be delegated to intelligent systems. Administrative work, data organization, scheduling, and preliminary drafts are prime candidates for automation. Delegating these tasks frees mental bandwidth for strategy and innovation. However, automation must remain supervised to preserve authenticity and accuracy. The entrepreneur retains final oversight to ensure alignment with brand voice and values. When balanced correctly, automation enhances rather than replaces human judgment. Effort decreases while output increases. The engine operates smoothly because energy is directed toward high-impact decisions instead of repetitive chores.

An effective productivity engine integrates feedback loops that encourage continuous improvement. AI enables entrepreneurs to measure performance in real time rather than waiting for quarterly reviews. Data from marketing campaigns, product launches, and customer interactions informs refinements quickly. Each cycle of execution generates insights that feed into the next iteration. This loop shortens the distance between experiment and optimization. Entrepreneurs no longer rely on guesswork when adjusting offers or messaging. Instead, they leverage intelligent analysis to guide improvements strategically. The engine becomes adaptive rather than rigid. Continuous feedback ensures that productivity evolves with market conditions. Growth accelerates because learning happens within the workflow itself.

Time management transforms dramatically once the AI productivity engine is operational. Tasks that once consumed entire mornings can be completed within focused intervals. Entrepreneurs gain structured blocks for strategic thinking rather than reacting to constant interruptions. AI handles background processes while the operator concentrates on high-leverage decisions. This structured environment increases confidence and reduces stress. Productivity becomes sustainable because energy is preserved rather than depleted. Consistency emerges naturally when systems support execution. The entrepreneur moves from overwhelm to control. Each day builds upon the previous one without starting from zero. The engine generates momentum that carries forward instead of resetting.

Collaboration between human creativity and machine efficiency defines the most powerful productivity engines. AI excels at processing information, generating drafts, and identifying patterns. Humans excel at judgment, storytelling, and emotional nuance. When these strengths combine, workflows reach a new level of sophistication. The entrepreneur guides AI with clear prompts and refined criteria. AI responds with structured outputs that accelerate refinement. This partnership creates a compounding effect where ideas move swiftly from concept to completion. The engine becomes a collaborative ecosystem rather than a static toolset. Productivity feels amplified rather than automated. The result is work that maintains authenticity while achieving scale.

Scalability is embedded within the productivity engine when workflows are designed with growth in mind. Entrepreneurs should build systems that handle increased demand without collapsing under pressure. AI allows replication of successful processes across new products or markets. Templates, prompts, and structured sequences can be reused and refined over time. This reuse reduces startup time for future initiatives. As revenue grows, the engine accommodates expansion without proportional increases in workload. Scalability ensures that productivity improvements translate into long-term income growth. The entrepreneur avoids burnout while pursuing ambition. The engine supports upward momentum without sacrificing balance. Growth becomes strategic rather than chaotic.

Accountability strengthens the productivity engine because measurement reinforces discipline. Entrepreneurs must track outputs, conversion rates, and engagement metrics consistently. AI simplifies tracking by consolidating information into accessible dashboards and summaries. Regular evaluation identifies bottlenecks that hinder performance. Adjustments can then be implemented quickly within established workflows. Accountability prevents complacency and maintains forward progress. The entrepreneur treats productivity as a measurable system rather than a subjective feeling. Clear metrics transform daily effort into visible results. This transparency encourages continued refinement and motivation. The engine thrives on measurable momentum.

Building an AI productivity engine ultimately empowers the everyday entrepreneur to operate with precision and confidence. Instead of chasing scattered opportunities, they execute within structured systems designed for profitability. Output multiplies because workflows eliminate inefficiencies and preserve energy. Effort decreases because automation absorbs repetitive burdens. Consistency increases because repeatable cycles replace improvisation. The entrepreneur transitions from reactive work to proactive strategy. AI becomes a dependable partner rather than an overwhelming novelty. Daily income emerges from disciplined application of intelligent systems. Momentum compounds as each workflow reinforces the next. The productivity engine stands as the backbone of sustainable growth, proving that when smart tools are organized with clarity and intention, ordinary effort transforms into extraordinary results.

6

AI CONTENT THAT ATTRACTS BUYERS

Attention is the gateway to revenue, and in a digital economy saturated with noise, attracting buyers requires precision rather than volume. Artificial intelligence has transformed content creation from a time-consuming obligation into a strategic advantage for everyday entrepreneurs. Yet tools alone do not attract buyers; intentional positioning does. AI content that converts begins with clarity about who the message is for and what problem it addresses. When entrepreneurs understand their audience's pain points, aspirations, and language, AI becomes a powerful amplifier of relevance. Instead of producing generic posts, they craft targeted messaging that feels personal and timely. The goal is not to impress algorithms but to resonate with humans. AI accelerates research, drafts messaging, and refines structure, but emotional intelligence drives connection. The entrepreneur's voice guides the tone while AI enhances efficiency. When clarity meets consistency, content stops being filler and becomes a revenue-driving asset.

Marketing content must serve a defined purpose within a broader system rather than exist as isolated output. Many entrepreneurs create posts, emails, and videos without a conversion pathway in place. AI helps design content sequences that move buyers from awareness to trust to action. Each piece becomes part of a larger narrative rather than a standalone effort. Educational material builds credibility, storytelling builds relatability, and calls to action build momentum. AI can map these sequences quickly, ensuring strategic alignment across platforms. Instead of guessing what to publish next, entrepreneurs follow structured workflows. This systematic approach transforms creativity into a measurable business driver. Buyers respond to clarity and consistency over sporadic brilliance. Content that converts is content engineered with intention.

Authority assets are essential for standing out in competitive markets, and AI accelerates their development dramatically. Ebooks, white papers, case studies, and in-depth guides establish expertise that differentiates entrepreneurs from casual creators. AI assists with research, outline generation, and draft refinement, reducing production time significantly. However, authenticity remains critical, so the entrepreneur shapes the final message with personal insight and perspective. Authority grows when knowledge is delivered with confidence and clarity. Buyers are more likely to trust those who demonstrate depth rather than surface-level commentary. AI enables rapid compilation of insights that would otherwise require extensive manual effort. This efficiency allows entrepreneurs to publish consistently without sacrificing substance. Authority compounds over time as content libraries expand. When credibility increases, conversion rates follow naturally.

Search visibility remains a powerful driver of inbound

interest, and AI enhances search optimization processes. Entrepreneurs can analyze keyword trends, competitor positioning, and search intent quickly. AI suggests content structures aligned with what audiences actively seek. This alignment increases the likelihood that material will appear in relevant search results. However, search optimization must balance data with genuine value. Content written solely for algorithms often lacks engagement and fails to convert. AI helps bridge the gap by generating drafts optimized for both readability and discoverability. The entrepreneur ensures that insights remain actionable and clear. Search-driven content acts as a long-term asset, attracting prospects consistently. Visibility built on value creates sustainable lead generation.

Storytelling remains one of the most powerful conversion tools available to entrepreneurs. AI can assist in organizing narratives, refining tone, and identifying emotional triggers within messaging. Stories humanize brands and make abstract solutions tangible. Buyers connect with experiences and transformations more deeply than with technical descriptions. Entrepreneurs who integrate personal stories or customer journeys into content create memorable impressions. AI enhances storytelling by suggesting structure and pacing while preserving authenticity. Each story becomes a bridge between problem and solution. When buyers see themselves reflected in narratives, trust strengthens. Conversion becomes a natural extension of emotional connection. AI content that includes storytelling outperforms content that relies solely on features.

Consistency separates successful content strategies from short-lived bursts of visibility. AI reduces the workload associated with maintaining regular output across multiple platforms. Entrepreneurs can repurpose core ideas into blogs, social media posts, emails, and scripts efficiently. This repurposing maximizes reach without multiplying effort. Consistency builds familiarity, and familiarity builds trust over time. Buyers are more inclined to engage with brands they encounter repeatedly. AI ensures that messaging remains cohesive while adapting to platform-specific nuances. Structured content calendars supported by intelligent tools maintain momentum. The entrepreneur's role becomes strategic oversight rather than constant creation from scratch. Sustainable consistency fuels predictable growth.

Personalization increases engagement dramatically, and AI makes personalization scalable for everyday entrepreneurs. Tailoring messages to specific segments once required advanced marketing teams. Today, individuals can use AI to adjust tone, examples, and offers for different audience groups. Personalized emails, targeted ads, and segmented campaigns increase relevance and response rates. Buyers respond positively when communication feels tailored rather than generic. AI assists in analyzing behavior patterns to refine targeting strategies. This precision reduces wasted effort and increases conversion efficiency. Entrepreneurs can nurture relationships with prospects at different stages of the buyer journey. Personalization transforms mass communication into meaningful interaction. When relevance increases, trust and revenue follow.

Calls to action determine whether content generates income or remains informational. AI helps craft compelling calls that encourage immediate response without feeling aggressive. Clear instructions guide buyers toward next steps, whether scheduling a consultation or purchasing a product. Effective calls are specific, benefit-focused, and aligned with audience readiness. AI can test variations to identify which phrasing yields stronger engagement. Entrepreneurs refine these calls through ongoing analysis and iteration. A subtle shift in wording can significantly impact conversion rates. Strategic placement within content ensures visibility without disrupting flow. Conversion-focused content treats every interaction as an opportunity to move forward. AI supports precision in crafting these critical moments.

Metrics transform content creation from subjective creativity into measurable performance. AI simplifies tracking engagement rates, click-through rates, and conversion metrics. Entrepreneurs gain insight into which topics resonate most strongly. This data informs future content direction and investment of time. Instead of relying on intuition alone, decisions become evidence-based. Continuous measurement allows rapid optimization within established workflows. Underperforming content can be adjusted or replaced strategically. High-performing themes can be expanded into larger offerings. AI accelerates this analysis, ensuring feedback remains timely. Content evolves intelligently when guided by measurable outcomes.

AI content that attracts buyers ultimately reflects strategic integration rather than random output. Smart tools enhance research, drafting, optimization, and analysis, but intentional direction shapes results. Entrepreneurs who treat content as an asset-building process gain sustainable advantages. Marketing material becomes a system designed to attract, nurture, and convert consistently. Authority assets establish credibility, personalized messaging strengthens relationships, and optimized calls drive revenue. AI reduces friction while amplifying creative potential. The everyday entrepreneur gains capabilities once limited to large marketing teams. When smart tools are aligned with strategic vision, content becomes a powerful income generator. Buyers respond to clarity, authenticity, and consistency above all else. In this new era, AI-driven content does more than fill space; it builds trust, drives action, and transforms attention into daily income.

7

TURNING SKILLS INTO AI-POWERED SERVICES

Every entrepreneur possesses skills that seem ordinary to them but valuable to someone else. The challenge has never been having a skill; the challenge has been packaging it correctly and delivering it efficiently. Artificial intelligence changes the economics of service delivery by increasing output while decreasing production time. Skills that once required hours of manual effort can now be enhanced, accelerated, and refined with intelligent tools. This transformation allows everyday entrepreneurs to reposition simple abilities as scalable services. Writing, research, organization, marketing insight, editing, data interpretation, and customer communication all become premium offerings when combined with AI leverage. The difference between a low-value freelancer and a high-value operator lies in structure and positioning. AI enables entrepreneurs to elevate what they already know into systems that produce consistent outcomes. Clients do not pay for effort; they pay for results delivered reliably. When skills are packaged strategically, ordinary capabilities become high-margin service opportunities.

The first step in turning skills into AI-powered services is identifying outcomes rather than tasks. Many service providers sell hours instead of solutions, which limits income potential. Clients are not searching for time spent; they are searching for measurable improvements in their business. AI allows entrepreneurs to accelerate delivery, making outcome-based pricing more profitable. Instead of offering content writing by the hour, an operator can offer lead-generating content systems. Instead of offering general marketing advice, an entrepreneur can offer structured campaign blueprints supported by AI optimization. The focus shifts from labor to leverage. This repositioning transforms perception in the marketplace. Clients value services tied directly to revenue or efficiency gains. AI supports the backend execution while the entrepreneur communicates strategic value. Packaging outcomes elevates simple skills into premium offerings.

Once outcomes are defined, clarity in service structure becomes essential. A well-designed AI-powered service includes defined steps, timelines, deliverables, and communication checkpoints. AI can help standardize onboarding documents, questionnaires, and project outlines. This structure builds trust because clients understand exactly what to expect. Standardization also increases efficiency by reducing decision fatigue for the entrepreneur. Repeatable service frameworks allow faster delivery without sacrificing customization. AI assists with research, drafting, and refinement within each structured phase. The entrepreneur oversees quality control and strategic direction. This combination ensures consistency across multiple clients. Structured services feel professional and dependable. Clients return repeatedly when experiences are predictable and results are reliable.

Automation enhances service delivery by reducing repetitive manual work. Many service providers waste energy recreating processes for each new client. AI-powered templates, prompts, and workflows eliminate unnecessary duplication. For example, a consultant can use AI to generate personalized strategy summaries based on standardized inputs. A content specialist can create adaptable frameworks that adjust for different industries. Automation frees time for deeper analysis and creative problem-solving. Clients benefit from faster turnaround times and clearer deliverables. The entrepreneur benefits from increased capacity without increased stress. Automation does not remove personalization; it streamlines preparation so personalization can be more intentional. AI transforms backend complexity into front-end simplicity. The service becomes both scalable and refined.

Pricing strategy determines whether AI-powered services remain sustainable long term. Entrepreneurs often undervalue their work because they measure effort rather than impact. AI reduces production time, but the value delivered remains significant. Pricing should reflect transformation, efficiency gains, and measurable business outcomes. When clients experience clear improvements, repeat engagement becomes natural. Recurring service models, such as monthly optimization or content management packages, create predictable revenue streams. AI supports recurring models by maintaining quality across ongoing deliverables. Subscription-based services build long-term relationships rather than one-time transactions. Entrepreneurs who price strategically position themselves as partners rather than temporary contractors. Repeated value delivery strengthens trust and loyalty. Sustainable income emerges when pricing aligns with results rather than hours.

Marketing AI-powered services requires clear articulation of differentiation. As more entrepreneurs adopt AI tools, generic services become crowded quickly. Differentiation emerges from specialization, clarity of outcome, and personal perspective. An entrepreneur might specialize in helping real estate agents automate lead follow-up or assist authors with AI-enhanced publishing strategies. Narrow positioning reduces competition while increasing perceived expertise. AI supports niche-specific research and messaging development. Clients are drawn to specialists who understand their context deeply. Clear differentiation simplifies marketing efforts because messaging speaks directly to defined audiences. Authority grows when focus remains consistent. AI enhances delivery, but positioning determines visibility.

Trust remains the foundation of high-value service relationships. Clients must feel confident that AI enhances quality rather than replacing thoughtful expertise. Transparency about process builds credibility. Entrepreneurs can explain how AI accelerates research and drafting while human oversight ensures strategic alignment. Demonstrating examples, case studies, and measurable results reinforces trust. AI can assist in compiling performance reports and visual summaries for clients. Clear communication ensures expectations are managed effectively. When clients see evidence of improvement, confidence increases naturally. Trust converts one-time engagements into recurring contracts. AI-powered services thrive when transparency and accountability are embedded within the process.

Scaling AI-powered services requires disciplined workflow management. Entrepreneurs must balance automation with oversight to maintain quality as volume increases. AI enables expansion by handling preliminary research, drafting, and formatting tasks efficiently. However, strategic decisions remain under human control. Delegating certain stages to subcontractors may become feasible once systems are well defined. AI ensures consistent guidelines across all contributors. Scaling becomes less about hiring rapidly and more about refining systems intelligently. Growth occurs without sacrificing client experience. Entrepreneurs who design scalable frameworks avoid burnout while expanding revenue. Sustainable scaling depends on clarity and structure rather than sheer effort.

Client retention becomes significantly easier when services integrate continuous optimization. AI provides ongoing analysis of performance metrics and customer behavior. Entrepreneurs can proactively recommend adjustments before clients request changes. This proactive approach positions the service provider as a strategic partner. Recurring reviews demonstrate commitment to long-term success rather than short-term delivery. Clients value guidance that evolves with market shifts. AI simplifies monitoring trends and identifying opportunities. Continuous improvement strengthens loyalty and justifies premium pricing. Retention reduces acquisition costs and stabilizes cash flow. AI-powered services become indispensable when improvement feels ongoing. Long-term partnerships replace transactional engagements.

Turning skills into AI-powered services ultimately transforms the everyday entrepreneur into a strategic operator. What once felt limited by time becomes amplified by intelligent leverage. Simple abilities gain exponential reach when structured into repeatable systems. Clients pay repeatedly for clarity, consistency, and measurable improvement.

AI enhances research, production, and analysis while the entrepreneur directs vision and judgment. Packaging, positioning, pricing, and process design determine profitability more than raw talent. The operator who integrates AI thoughtfully gains competitive advantage without overwhelming complexity. Sustainable income emerges from disciplined execution supported by intelligent tools. Everyday entrepreneurs can compete with agencies and larger firms through precision and agility. When skills are organized into high-value frameworks and powered by AI efficiency, daily income transforms into recurring revenue built on expertise and trust.

8

CREATING DIGITAL PRODUCTS AT SCALE

Digital products represent one of the most powerful income models available to everyday entrepreneurs because they separate effort from earnings. Unlike services that require constant involvement, digital assets continue generating revenue long after creation. Artificial intelligence accelerates the process of building these products, turning ideas into structured offerings with remarkable efficiency. Entrepreneurs no longer need large teams or advanced technical expertise to produce professional materials. AI assists with research, outlining, drafting, editing, and formatting, reducing the time between concept and launch. This shift transforms digital product creation from a long-term project into a repeatable system. The goal is not simply to create content but to create value that solves specific problems consistently. Products that sell while you sleep are built on clarity, usefulness, and accessibility. AI amplifies the entrepreneur's ability to deliver these qualities at scale. When leveraged strategically, digital products become the foundation of sustainable passive income.

The first principle of creating digital products at scale

is understanding the problem-solution relationship. Buyers do not purchase ebooks or templates because they want more information; they buy because they want results faster. AI helps entrepreneurs identify common pain points by analyzing trends, search behavior, and customer questions. This insight guides product development toward real demand instead of assumptions. A focused problem creates a focused product, which increases conversion rates significantly. Entrepreneurs should aim for specificity rather than broad coverage. AI can help refine the scope so the product feels practical and immediately useful. Clear outcomes make marketing easier because benefits are obvious. When buyers understand exactly what they will gain, hesitation decreases. Successful digital products begin with solving one clear problem exceptionally well.

Ebooks remain one of the most accessible entry points for digital product creation. AI streamlines the writing process by assisting with outlines, chapter expansion, and structural consistency. Entrepreneurs can move from idea to finished manuscript faster than ever before. However, speed should never replace depth or clarity. AI-generated drafts must be refined with human insight to ensure authenticity and relevance. A strong ebook provides actionable steps rather than vague inspiration. Formatting, design, and readability also influence perceived value. AI tools help optimize layout and improve visual presentation without expensive software. When positioned correctly, ebooks establish authority while generating income. They become both revenue streams and marketing assets that attract future buyers.

Guides and playbooks offer another powerful digital product category because they focus on implementation. Buyers often struggle not with knowledge but with execution. AI helps entrepreneurs transform complex processes into step-by-step frameworks that feel manageable. Structured guides reduce overwhelm and increase user satisfaction. Entrepreneurs can use AI to create checklists, examples, and actionable workflows quickly. These elements increase the practical value of the product. Guides that produce measurable outcomes encourage repeat purchases and referrals. AI allows rapid updating as trends and tools evolve. This adaptability ensures products remain relevant over time. A well-crafted guide positions the entrepreneur as a trusted problem solver.

Templates represent one of the highest-leverage digital products because they save buyers time immediately. AI enables entrepreneurs to generate templates for marketing, productivity, planning, and communication efficiently. Buyers appreciate resources that remove decision-making friction from their daily work. Templates transform abstract advice into concrete tools users can apply instantly. Entrepreneurs can bundle templates into themed packages that increase perceived value. AI assists in creating variations tailored to different industries or audiences. This customization expands market reach without requiring entirely new products. Templates often lead to repeat sales because satisfied customers seek additional resources. Simplicity becomes a selling point when execution feels effortless. Digital templates create ongoing revenue with minimal maintenance.

Systems-based digital products combine multiple elements into comprehensive solutions. These products might include ebooks, templates, video explanations, and workflows bundled together. AI supports the organization and integration of these components into cohesive systems. Buyers are willing to pay premium prices for solutions that feel complete. Entrepreneurs who package knowledge into structured systems position themselves as strategic experts rather than content creators. AI assists in maintaining consistency across all materials. Systems-based products reduce customer confusion by guiding users step by step. The more complete the solution, the higher the perceived value. These products often become flagship offerings within a business. Systems scale effectively because they deliver transformation rather than isolated information.

Automation plays a critical role in ensuring digital products truly sell while the entrepreneur sleeps. AI-powered marketing workflows can handle email sequences, customer onboarding, and follow-up communication automatically. Sales funnels guide buyers from awareness to purchase without constant manual involvement. Entrepreneurs design the system once and refine it through ongoing data analysis. AI helps optimize messaging and timing to increase conversion rates. Automated delivery ensures customers receive products instantly, improving satisfaction. This seamless experience reinforces professionalism and trust. Automation also frees entrepreneurs to focus on creating new products or improving existing ones. Revenue continues flowing even during downtime. The combination of automation and digital assets creates scalable income potential.

Marketing digital products effectively requires clear messaging that emphasizes outcomes rather than features. AI assists in crafting persuasive copy that speaks directly to buyer needs. Entrepreneurs can test different headlines, descriptions, and promotional angles quickly. Data-driven iteration improves performance over time. Content marketing supported by AI helps attract organic traffic through blogs, videos, and social media posts. Each piece of content becomes a pathway toward product sales. Consistent visibility builds familiarity, which increases trust. AI ensures marketing efforts remain efficient and aligned with audience interests. The goal is to create a steady flow of qualified buyers rather than sporadic spikes in sales. Effective marketing turns digital products into reliable income streams.

Scaling digital product creation requires a mindset shift from one-time projects to repeatable systems. Entrepreneurs should develop workflows that allow rapid development of new offerings. AI enables reuse of research, frameworks, and content structures across multiple products. This reuse accelerates production while maintaining quality. A growing product ecosystem increases customer lifetime value. Buyers who trust one product are more likely to purchase additional offerings. AI helps identify opportunities for expansion based on customer feedback and market trends. Scaling becomes a natural extension of existing success rather than a separate challenge. Consistent creation builds momentum and authority simultaneously. Over time, a library of digital products becomes a powerful business asset.

Creating digital products at scale ultimately empowers everyday entrepreneurs to build income that is not limited by time. AI transforms the process from overwhelming to achievable by simplifying research, creation, and distribution. Ebooks, guides, templates, and systems become vehicles for delivering value efficiently. When products solve real problems and are marketed strategically, sales continue long after creation. Automation ensures delivery and follow-up occur seamlessly without constant oversight. Entrepreneurs gain freedom to innovate while revenue flows in the background. The key lies in focusing on outcomes, structuring products clearly, and refining based on feedback. AI amplifies creativity and productivity when guided with intention. Digital products become more than content; they become scalable assets that support long-term growth. In the AI-powered economy, the entrepreneur who builds systems that sell while they sleep creates not just income but enduring leverage that compounds year after year.

9

THE AI MARKETING MULTIPLIER

Marketing has always been the engine of revenue, yet for many everyday entrepreneurs it becomes the most exhausting and inconsistent part of business. Artificial intelligence changes that equation by transforming marketing from a manual grind into a scalable system. The AI Marketing Multiplier is not about replacing human connection but about amplifying it intelligently. When automation is designed strategically, promotion becomes steady rather than sporadic. Entrepreneurs no longer need to rely on bursts of energy to maintain visibility. Instead, they build systems that distribute value consistently across platforms. AI supports research, drafting, segmentation, scheduling, and optimization without diluting voice. The multiplier effect occurs when one core idea expands into multiple touchpoints automatically. Marketing shifts from reactive effort to proactive structure. When built correctly, AI-driven promotion increases reach while preserving authenticity and trust.

Automation begins with clarity about brand voice and positioning. Without defined messaging principles, automated content quickly feels generic or mechanical. Entrepreneurs must articulate tone, values, and audience expectations before implementing AI workflows. This foundational clarity ensures that every automated output aligns with identity. AI tools can then be trained or guided to replicate stylistic preferences consistently. Brand consistency builds familiarity, and familiarity builds trust. Automation becomes an extension of personality rather than a substitute for it. The entrepreneur maintains oversight while allowing intelligent systems to handle repetition. Clear voice guidelines act as guardrails that protect authenticity. When automation reflects identity accurately, scale enhances credibility rather than eroding it.

Content distribution is one of the most powerful applications of the AI marketing multiplier. A single piece of long-form content can be transformed into blog posts, social media updates, email newsletters, and short-form scripts. AI accelerates this repurposing process dramatically. Entrepreneurs gain broader exposure without multiplying workload. Consistent presence across platforms strengthens brand recall. AI scheduling tools ensure that content is published at optimal times for engagement. Instead of manually posting each update, entrepreneurs design distribution systems once and refine them periodically. This efficiency allows creative focus to remain on strategy rather than mechanics. Reach expands while effort stabilizes. Distribution becomes a steady engine of attention rather than an unpredictable task.

Personalized messaging elevates automation from mass broadcasting to meaningful engagement. AI enables segmentation based on behavior, preferences, and purchase history. Entrepreneurs can tailor email sequences and outreach messages to specific audience segments. This customization increases relevance and response rates. Buyers respond positively when communication feels thoughtful and targeted. AI simplifies the management of segmented campaigns without overwhelming complexity. Personalization no longer requires a large marketing department. Everyday entrepreneurs can deliver nuanced messaging at scale. Trust strengthens when buyers feel understood rather than marketed to. Automation guided by empathy transforms outreach into relationship building.

Lead generation becomes more efficient when AI supports research and targeting. Entrepreneurs can identify high-probability prospects through data analysis rather than guesswork. AI tools assist in crafting outreach messages that align with prospect interests. Automated follow-up sequences ensure consistent communication without manual tracking. This structured approach reduces missed opportunities. Outreach feels organized and professional rather than sporadic. Entrepreneurs maintain visibility in prospect inboxes without becoming intrusive. AI analyzes response patterns to refine future messaging. Each campaign improves through iterative learning. The multiplier effect emerges as outreach efforts compound steadily over time.

Advertising campaigns benefit significantly from AI optimization capabilities. Entrepreneurs can test variations of headlines, visuals, and calls to action rapidly. AI analyzes performance metrics and suggests adjustments for higher conversion rates. This iterative process increases return on investment. Instead of relying solely on intuition, entrepreneurs make data-driven decisions. Automation manages budget allocation and audience targeting efficiently. Campaign performance improves without constant manual monitoring. AI provides insights that would otherwise require advanced analytical expertise. Entrepreneurs remain strategic directors while AI handles computational complexity. Advertising becomes a disciplined experiment rather than a gamble.

Maintaining authenticity requires intentional transparency about automation practices. Entrepreneurs should ensure that automated responses do not feel deceptive or robotic. Clear communication about availability and response times sets realistic expectations. AI can draft responses quickly, but final review ensures tone and accuracy. Trust erodes when automation appears careless or impersonal. The goal is to enhance responsiveness while preserving sincerity. Entrepreneurs must periodically audit automated sequences to confirm alignment with evolving brand values. Consistency and empathy remain non-negotiable. Automation supports human connection but cannot replace genuine care. Authenticity remains the foundation upon which all marketing efforts rest.

Analytics play a crucial role in maximizing the AI marketing multiplier. AI consolidates performance data from multiple channels into accessible dashboards. Entrepreneurs gain real-time visibility into engagement, conversion, and retention metrics. This transparency enables rapid adjustment of strategies. Underperforming campaigns can be modified without delay. High-performing content can be expanded strategically. Data-driven iteration strengthens marketing efficiency. Entrepreneurs move from reactive corrections to proactive optimization. Each metric informs smarter decisions about allocation of effort and resources. Continuous analysis transforms marketing into a measurable growth engine.

Community engagement benefits from AI-supported moderation and content scheduling. Entrepreneurs can maintain active online communities without constant presence. AI assists in responding to frequently asked questions and organizing discussions. This responsiveness fosters a sense of attentiveness and professionalism. However, periodic personal interaction remains essential for credibility. Automation handles structure while entrepreneurs contribute depth. Community members appreciate both efficiency and authenticity. Consistent engagement strengthens loyalty and word-of-mouth referrals. AI ensures that engagement does not lapse during busy periods. The multiplier effect extends beyond content into relationships.

The AI marketing multiplier ultimately empowers everyday entrepreneurs to operate with strategic precision and sustainable momentum. Automation transforms promotion from a draining obligation into a disciplined system. Messaging remains authentic because clarity of voice guides implementation. Outreach becomes consistent and personalized through intelligent segmentation. Advertising campaigns improve through iterative data analysis. Community engagement thrives under structured support. Entrepreneurs reclaim time while expanding reach and influence. Trust remains intact because automation enhances rather than replaces sincerity. When smart tools are integrated thoughtfully, marketing scales without sacrificing humanity. In this new era, the entrepreneur who masters the AI marketing multiplier builds visibility, credibility, and revenue simultaneously, proving that automation and authenticity can coexist powerfully when guided by clear vision and disciplined execution.

10

SIMPLE SALES SYSTEMS FOR DAILY INCOME

Sales systems are the heartbeat of any profitable business, yet many everyday entrepreneurs treat sales as an unpredictable event instead of a structured process. Artificial intelligence changes this dynamic by enabling entrepreneurs to design simple, repeatable pathways that guide buyers toward decisions naturally. A sales system does not need to be complex to be effective; it needs clarity, consistency, and intentional design. The purpose of a funnel is to reduce friction between curiosity and commitment. AI helps entrepreneurs understand customer behavior, refine messaging, and optimize every stage of the buyer journey. Instead of guessing what works, operators can build systems informed by real data and continuous feedback. Consistent revenue emerges when sales pathways operate even when the entrepreneur is focused elsewhere. The goal is not aggressive selling but intelligent guidance that helps buyers make confident choices. AI supports this approach by simplifying communication and automation. When sales become systematic rather than emotional, daily income becomes predictable.

The foundation of a simple sales system begins with a clear and compelling offer. Buyers must immediately understand what they are getting and why it matters. AI assists entrepreneurs in refining value propositions by analyzing language that resonates with target audiences. A strong offer solves a specific problem and communicates outcomes rather than features. Clarity reduces hesitation and increases conversion rates significantly. Entrepreneurs often overcomplicate offers by adding unnecessary options or confusing language. AI helps simplify messaging so benefits stand out clearly. The best offers feel obvious and easy to accept. When buyers see immediate relevance, the sales process feels natural rather than forced. A clear offer becomes the anchor point around which the entire funnel operates.

Funnels organize the buyer journey into structured stages that move prospects from awareness to purchase. The first stage focuses on attracting attention through valuable content or lead magnets. AI enables rapid creation of targeted materials that align with audience interests. These entry points should provide genuine value while introducing the entrepreneur's expertise. The next stage builds trust through education, storytelling, and proof of results. AI assists in crafting email sequences and follow-up messages that maintain engagement. As trust increases, prospects become more receptive to offers. Each step in the funnel should feel like a logical progression rather than a sudden sales push. Simplicity ensures that prospects do not feel overwhelmed. A well-designed funnel turns strangers into buyers through consistent guidance.

Lead magnets play a crucial role in generating consistent pipeline activity. These resources might include guides, templates, checklists, or short training materials that solve immediate problems. AI helps entrepreneurs develop lead magnets quickly while maintaining quality and relevance. The purpose is to exchange value for contact information, creating opportunities for ongoing communication. Effective lead magnets attract qualified prospects rather than casual browsers. AI can analyze which topics generate the strongest engagement and adjust accordingly. Once leads enter the system, automated nurturing sequences keep them engaged. This ongoing communication builds familiarity and trust over time. Entrepreneurs who consistently capture leads create a predictable flow of potential buyers. Lead magnets transform passive traffic into active opportunities.

Email marketing remains one of the most effective conversion tools within simple sales systems. AI enhances email strategy by optimizing subject lines, content structure, and timing. Automated sequences allow entrepreneurs to nurture relationships without constant manual effort. Emails should educate, inspire, and guide rather than pressure. Story-driven communication strengthens emotional connection and reinforces credibility. AI assists in personalizing messages based on behavior and preferences. Segmented email flows increase relevance and engagement rates. Consistency in communication ensures that prospects remain connected to the brand. Over time, trust deepens and resistance decreases. Email sequences become a quiet but powerful engine driving daily income.

Conversion pathways must remove unnecessary friction to encourage action. Complicated checkout processes or unclear calls to action reduce sales significantly. AI helps identify drop-off points within funnels by analyzing user behavior. Entrepreneurs can simplify forms, clarify instructions, and streamline navigation based on insights. Clear calls to action guide buyers toward next steps confidently. Every page within the funnel should answer potential objections proactively. Testimonials, case studies, and guarantees strengthen confidence during decision-making. AI can assist in testing variations to determine which elements improve conversions. Small adjustments often produce significant results. Simplified pathways make purchasing feel effortless rather than stressful.

Upsells and downsells increase revenue without requiring additional traffic. Once a buyer commits, they are more open to related offers that enhance their results. AI helps identify complementary products or services that align naturally with the initial purchase. Strategic upsells add value rather than appearing opportunistic. Downsells provide alternatives for buyers who hesitate at higher price points. This layered approach ensures that opportunities are not lost unnecessarily. AI can automate offer sequencing based on customer behavior. Entrepreneurs maximize lifetime value while maintaining customer satisfaction. Revenue increases without increasing marketing costs. Smart offer stacking turns single transactions into expanded income streams.

Data-driven optimization keeps sales systems effective as markets evolve. AI analyzes conversion rates, click patterns, and customer feedback continuously. Entrepreneurs gain insights into which stages perform well and which require adjustment. This feedback loop enables ongoing refinement without guesswork. A sales system should never remain static; it must adapt based on real-world results. AI accelerates testing and iteration by identifying patterns quickly. Entrepreneurs can experiment with headlines, pricing, and messaging confidently. Continuous improvement ensures long-term profitability. Small optimizations compound over time into significant revenue growth. The system becomes stronger with each iteration.

Trust remains the most valuable currency within any sales system. Automation and AI should enhance trust rather than undermine it. Honest messaging, realistic promises, and consistent delivery build long-term relationships. Buyers who feel respected are more likely to return and recommend others. AI assists in maintaining responsiveness and consistency across communication channels. However, human oversight ensures empathy and authenticity remain central. Entrepreneurs who prioritize customer outcomes over short-term gains build stronger brands. Trust reduces sales resistance and increases referral-driven growth. A trustworthy system generates revenue naturally without aggressive tactics. Long-term success depends on credibility more than cleverness.

Simple sales systems for daily income ultimately empower everyday entrepreneurs to move from uncertainty to predictability. Funnels guide prospects through structured journeys that feel natural and supportive. Offers communicate clear value and solve real problems. Automation maintains consistent communication while reducing manual workload. AI enhances every stage through analysis, optimization, and personalization. Conversion pathways remove friction and encourage confident decisions. Upsells and retention strategies expand customer lifetime value. Data-driven refinement keeps systems aligned with evolving markets. Trust anchors the entire process, ensuring sustainability and loyalty. When entrepreneurs build simple, intentional sales systems supported by AI, revenue stops feeling accidental and starts flowing consistently, proving that daily income is not a matter of luck but the result of disciplined design and intelligent execution.

11

AUTOMATION WITHOUT LOSING CONTROL

Automation promises freedom, yet many entrepreneurs hesitate because they fear losing control over quality, voice, and brand identity. Artificial intelligence amplifies this tension by making automation more powerful than ever before. The key is understanding that automation should serve strategy, not replace judgment. Everyday entrepreneurs must approach automation as a partnership between human direction and machine execution. Control is not lost when systems are designed intentionally; it is strengthened through clarity and structure. AI can handle repetitive tasks, but entrepreneurs remain responsible for standards and vision. The goal is not to remove human influence but to protect it by eliminating unnecessary workload. When automation is aligned with clear principles, consistency actually improves. Entrepreneurs gain the ability to scale without sacrificing what makes their brand unique. Automation without losing control begins with defining non-negotiable values that guide every system.

The first step in intelligent automation is identifying

which tasks truly deserve automation. Not every activity should be delegated to AI. Repetitive, predictable, and time-consuming tasks are ideal candidates because they drain energy without requiring deep creativity. Administrative work, data organization, scheduling, and preliminary drafts often fall into this category. Strategic decision-making, emotional storytelling, and relationship-building should remain human-led. Entrepreneurs who automate indiscriminately risk producing content that feels generic or disconnected. AI should handle execution while humans provide direction and refinement. Clear boundaries protect authenticity and ensure quality remains high. Automation becomes empowering when it removes friction without removing personality. The strongest systems are built on intentional delegation rather than blind automation.

Brand voice represents one of the most valuable assets an entrepreneur possesses. AI can replicate patterns, but it cannot originate identity without guidance. Entrepreneurs must define tone, language style, and messaging principles before automating content creation. These guidelines act as a blueprint that AI follows consistently. Reviewing outputs ensures alignment with brand expectations. Over time, AI-generated drafts become more accurate as instructions become clearer. Consistency in voice builds familiarity, which strengthens trust with audiences. Automation should reinforce brand personality rather than dilute it. Entrepreneurs who treat voice as a strategic asset maintain differentiation even while scaling. Control remains intact because AI operates within clearly defined parameters.

Quality assurance becomes essential as automation increases output volume. Without review processes, mistakes or inconsistencies can multiply quickly. Entrepreneurs should implement checkpoints within automated workflows to verify accuracy and relevance. AI can assist in proofreading, formatting, and optimization, but final approval should remain human-driven. This oversight ensures that published materials meet established standards. Quality control protects reputation and prevents erosion of trust. Automated systems should be designed to flag potential issues rather than bypass scrutiny. Entrepreneurs who prioritize quality over speed maintain long-term credibility. Consistent excellence creates a competitive advantage that automation alone cannot replicate. Intelligent automation balances efficiency with careful oversight.

Automation also affects customer communication, which requires careful management to preserve authenticity. AI-powered responses can improve speed and consistency, but they must avoid sounding robotic. Entrepreneurs should craft templates that reflect genuine tone and empathy. Personalized touches within automated messages increase engagement and satisfaction. AI can assist in tailoring responses based on customer history or preferences. However, complex or emotionally sensitive interactions should transition to human attention. This balance ensures efficiency without sacrificing connection. Customers appreciate quick responses, but they value sincerity even more. Automation should enhance responsiveness while preserving warmth. Control is maintained when entrepreneurs decide where automation ends and human interaction begins.

Workflow design plays a central role in maintaining control over automated systems. Entrepreneurs should map processes step by step before introducing AI tools. Clear workflows prevent confusion and ensure that automation supports specific outcomes. Each stage should have defined inputs, outputs, and review checkpoints. AI thrives within structured environments where expectations are explicit. Well-designed workflows reduce errors and improve consistency across projects. Entrepreneurs gain visibility into how tasks move through the system. This transparency reinforces confidence and reduces anxiety about losing oversight. Automation becomes predictable rather than chaotic. Structured workflows turn AI into a reliable operational partner.

Data monitoring allows entrepreneurs to maintain control through measurable feedback. AI systems generate valuable insights about performance, engagement, and efficiency. Entrepreneurs should regularly review analytics to ensure automation aligns with business goals. Metrics reveal whether content resonates, campaigns convert, or workflows remain efficient. Adjustments can be made quickly when performance declines. Continuous monitoring transforms automation into an adaptive system rather than a static setup. Entrepreneurs remain in control because decisions are informed by real data. AI provides visibility that manual processes often lack. Performance tracking ensures that automation drives improvement rather than complacency. Data-informed oversight strengthens confidence in scaling efforts.

Scalability is one of the greatest advantages of automation, but scaling without discipline creates risk. Entrepreneurs should expand automation gradually, testing systems before applying them broadly. Incremental growth allows refinement and reduces the chance of large-scale errors. AI can replicate successful processes rapidly once proven effective. This measured approach preserves quality while increasing capacity. Entrepreneurs avoid overwhelm because systems evolve intentionally. Scalability becomes sustainable when grounded in tested workflows. Control remains strong because expansion follows evidence rather than impulse. AI amplifies what already works instead of magnifying weaknesses. Gradual scaling builds confidence and long-term stability.

Ethical considerations also influence automation decisions. Entrepreneurs must ensure that AI-generated content remains honest, accurate, and respectful. Misleading automation damages trust and reputation quickly. Transparency about automated processes fosters credibility with audiences. Entrepreneurs should avoid overpromising or creating false impressions through automated messaging. Ethical guidelines serve as safeguards against unintended consequences. AI should reflect the values of the business rather than undermine them. Responsible automation strengthens long-term relationships with customers. Trust grows when audiences feel respected and informed. Control includes not only operational oversight but moral responsibility as well.

Automation without losing control ultimately empowers everyday entrepreneurs to operate with greater precision, consistency, and confidence. AI removes repetitive burdens while preserving the human elements that define successful brands. Quality remains high because review processes and clear standards guide execution. Voice stays authentic because entrepreneurs define and protect identity intentionally. Customer relationships strengthen when automation supports responsiveness without replacing empathy. Structured workflows and data monitoring provide visibility that reinforces control. Scaling becomes achievable without sacrificing integrity or trust. Entrepreneurs move from feeling overwhelmed to feeling empowered by intelligent systems. Automation becomes a tool for amplification rather than substitution. When guided with clarity and discipline, AI allows entrepreneurs to expand their reach while keeping their hands firmly on the steering wheel, proving that true control is not about doing everything manually but about designing systems that protect what matters most.

12

SCALING FROM SIDE INCOME TO REAL BUSINESS

Every successful business begins as a small experiment, often born from late nights, limited resources, and cautious optimism. What starts as side income can eventually grow into a full-scale operation, but the transition requires intentional strategy rather than accidental growth. Artificial intelligence accelerates this journey by helping entrepreneurs operate efficiently long before they hire teams or invest heavily. The challenge is knowing when to shift from part-time execution to full business commitment. Scaling too early can create instability, while scaling too late can limit momentum. Entrepreneurs must recognize the signals that indicate readiness for expansion. Consistent revenue, repeat customers, and predictable workflows are key indicators. AI helps reveal these patterns through data and analytics. Growth becomes less emotional and more measurable. Scaling from side income to real business begins with clarity about sustainability rather than excitement alone.

The first milestone in scaling is achieving consistency in income streams. Side projects often produce sporadic results, but real businesses generate reliable revenue patterns. Entrepreneurs should track monthly trends to identify stability before expanding aggressively. AI-powered dashboards and analytics tools make it easier to visualize performance over time. Consistency signals that the market values the offer and that systems are working. Without predictable income, scaling introduces unnecessary risk. Entrepreneurs must ensure that demand exists beyond temporary trends or isolated successes. AI assists in identifying recurring customer behavior and purchase cycles. Stable revenue creates confidence for reinvestment decisions. Consistency transforms a hobby into a viable enterprise foundation.

Expanding operations requires shifting from a creator mindset to an operator mindset. In the early stages, entrepreneurs handle everything personally. As demand grows, this approach becomes unsustainable. AI enables delegation without immediate hiring by automating repetitive tasks and standardizing workflows. Entrepreneurs can document processes and create systems that reduce dependency on personal effort. This transition protects energy and prevents burnout. Expansion should focus on strengthening infrastructure before increasing volume. Systems must support growth rather than collapse under pressure. AI provides scalability by maintaining efficiency across larger workloads. Operators think in terms of processes, not just tasks. This mindset shift is essential for long-term stability.

Pricing strategy becomes critical during the scaling phase because undervaluation limits growth potential. Many entrepreneurs maintain low prices out of fear of losing customers. However, higher pricing often reflects increased expertise, improved systems, and stronger results.

AI helps analyze competitor positioning and market expectations to guide pricing decisions. Entrepreneurs should gradually increase prices while communicating added value clearly. Premium pricing attracts more committed clients and reduces workload pressure. Scaling requires revenue per customer to grow alongside volume. AI-supported performance tracking provides evidence of results that justify price adjustments. Confident pricing reinforces brand positioning. Sustainable businesses prioritize value-based pricing rather than volume-driven survival.

Building a team becomes necessary when growth exceeds individual capacity. AI allows entrepreneurs to delay hiring by maximizing personal productivity, but eventually collaboration accelerates expansion. The key is hiring strategically rather than reactively. Entrepreneurs should first identify which tasks require human expertise versus AI automation. Clear systems and documentation make onboarding smoother. AI tools can assist with training materials, workflow guidance, and quality checks. Hiring should focus on roles that amplify strengths rather than duplicate effort. A lean, efficient team supported by AI often outperforms larger, disorganized operations. Leadership skills become increasingly important during this phase. Scaling successfully requires empowering others while maintaining clear direction.

Operational efficiency determines whether growth feels sustainable or chaotic. Entrepreneurs must refine workflows to handle increased demand without sacrificing quality. AI assists by automating scheduling, customer communication, and performance tracking. Standard operating procedures reduce errors and improve consistency. Efficiency creates space for strategic thinking rather than constant firefighting. Entrepreneurs should regularly review processes to eliminate bottlenecks. AI-generated insights highlight inefficiencies that might otherwise go unnoticed. Small adjustments compound into significant operational improvements. Efficient systems allow businesses to scale smoothly. Stability emerges when operations function predictably even during periods of rapid growth.

Customer retention becomes more important than customer acquisition during scaling. Acquiring new clients is expensive compared to serving existing ones effectively. AI helps track customer satisfaction, engagement, and purchasing behavior. Entrepreneurs can proactively address issues before they lead to churn. Loyalty programs, personalized communication, and ongoing value delivery strengthen relationships. Retained customers provide predictable revenue and valuable referrals. AI-powered segmentation enables tailored communication that feels personal at scale. Long-term stability depends on building trust rather than chasing constant new leads. Repeat customers validate the strength of the business model. Retention transforms growth into lasting stability.

Financial management evolves significantly as side income becomes a real business. Entrepreneurs must transition from informal tracking to structured financial oversight. AI tools simplify budgeting, forecasting, and expense analysis. Understanding cash flow becomes essential for confident decision-making. Expansion requires reinvestment in marketing, tools, and sometimes talent. Entrepreneurs should balance growth ambitions with financial prudence. AI-generated forecasts help anticipate seasonal fluctuations and plan accordingly. Clear financial visibility reduces stress and improves strategic planning. Sustainable scaling depends on disciplined financial habits. Profitability must remain a priority even during expansion phases.

Brand positioning strengthens during scaling as visibility and reputation increase. Entrepreneurs must ensure that messaging remains consistent across all touchpoints. AI supports content creation and distribution while maintaining brand voice. Authority-building activities such as publishing, speaking, or educational content reinforce credibility. A strong brand attracts higher-value clients and partnerships. Scaling should enhance brand identity rather than dilute it. Entrepreneurs must remain intentional about the audience they serve and the promises they make. AI assists in monitoring sentiment and engagement trends. Reputation becomes a valuable asset that supports long-term growth. Consistent branding builds trust that outlasts temporary market changes.

Scaling from side income to real business ultimately represents a transformation in identity as much as operations. Entrepreneurs move from experimenting to leading, from reacting to planning, and from surviving to building legacy. AI serves as a multiplier that supports this transition by increasing efficiency, clarity, and scalability. Expansion succeeds when systems, pricing, operations, and mindset evolve together. Long-term stability comes from balancing growth with discipline. Entrepreneurs who scale intentionally avoid the chaos that often accompanies rapid success. Consistent revenue, clear systems, and strong customer relationships create resilience against market shifts. AI empowers everyday entrepreneurs to compete with larger organizations while maintaining agility. The journey from side income to real business is not defined by a single leap but by deliberate steps supported by intelligent tools. When entrepreneurs expand with clarity and purpose, they build businesses that not only grow but endure, creating lasting income and meaningful impact for years to come.

13

THE AI OPERATOR'S LONG-TERM PLAYBOOK

The pace of technological change has accelerated beyond anything previous generations experienced, and artificial intelligence sits at the center of that transformation. Entrepreneurs who treat AI as a temporary advantage will eventually be overtaken by those who build long-term systems around adaptability. The AI Operator's Long-Term Playbook is not about chasing every new tool but about building resilient strategies that remain effective as the landscape evolves. Profitability over time depends less on technology itself and more on how entrepreneurs think about leverage, learning, and execution. Tools will change, interfaces will improve, and competitors will multiply, but principles of value creation remain stable. Everyday entrepreneurs must shift from short-term experimentation to long-term operational thinking. AI becomes a strategic layer woven into the foundation of business rather than a trend-driven add-on. The operator mindset focuses on sustainability rather than novelty. Long-term success comes from mastering systems that adapt without collapsing. Future-proofing begins when entrepreneurs stop asking what tool is newest and start asking what strategy endures.

Continuous learning forms the first pillar of long-term profitability in an AI-driven world. Technology evolves rapidly, and skills that feel advanced today may become standard tomorrow. Entrepreneurs who remain curious and committed to learning maintain a competitive edge. AI itself can accelerate education by summarizing research, analyzing trends, and suggesting new opportunities. Learning becomes integrated into daily workflows rather than a separate activity. Operators who dedicate time each week to exploration stay ahead of market shifts. This proactive approach prevents stagnation and complacency. Knowledge compounds over time just like financial investment. The entrepreneur who learns consistently adapts faster than competitors who resist change. Long-term profitability favors those who treat learning as a permanent responsibility rather than a temporary phase.

Diversification of income streams protects entrepreneurs from market volatility and tool dependency. Relying on a single platform or product creates vulnerability when algorithms change or trends fade. AI enables the creation of multiple revenue channels without overwhelming complexity. Digital products, services, subscriptions, consulting, and affiliate partnerships can coexist within one ecosystem. Each stream supports the others, creating stability even when one fluctuates. Diversification should be intentional rather than scattered. Operators design interconnected offers that serve the same audience in different ways. AI helps identify opportunities for expansion based on customer behavior. A diversified business absorbs shocks more effectively. Long-term operators build ecosystems instead of isolated offers.

Ownership of audience relationships becomes increasingly important as competition grows. Platforms change rules frequently, but direct access to customers remains a stable asset. Email lists, private communities, and owned content libraries create independence from external algorithms. AI assists in nurturing these relationships through personalized communication and segmentation. Entrepreneurs who prioritize audience ownership reduce long-term risk. Trust built directly with customers becomes a protective moat against competition. Operators focus on serving communities rather than chasing viral moments. Consistent value delivery strengthens loyalty over time. Audience ownership transforms marketing from constant acquisition into ongoing relationship management. Long-term profitability grows from trust that cannot be easily replicated.

Process documentation ensures scalability and resilience as businesses grow. Many entrepreneurs rely on memory and improvisation during early stages, which becomes problematic over time. AI helps document workflows, create guides, and maintain operational clarity. Documented systems allow businesses to adapt quickly when tools or team members change. Processes become assets that preserve knowledge and consistency. Operators treat systems as living frameworks that evolve with experience. Clear documentation reduces errors and onboarding time for future collaborators. AI can assist in updating and refining these materials efficiently. Structured processes protect businesses from disruption. Long-term stability emerges when operations are repeatable and transparent.

Innovation remains essential, but disciplined experimentation separates successful operators from distracted entrepreneurs. The market rewards those who test new ideas strategically rather than impulsively. AI allows rapid prototyping and validation without heavy investment. Operators run small experiments, measure outcomes, and scale what works. This approach reduces risk while encouraging continuous improvement. Experimentation becomes part of routine operations rather than a separate initiative. AI-generated insights guide decision-making and reduce guesswork. The key is balancing exploration with focus. Long-term operators innovate within a clear strategic framework. Sustainable growth comes from calculated experimentation rather than constant reinvention.

Brand reputation becomes more valuable as AI-generated content floods the marketplace. Authenticity and trust differentiate entrepreneurs in an environment where production volume is no longer rare. Operators focus on consistency, transparency, and delivering real value. AI can support brand messaging but cannot replace integrity. Long-term success depends on maintaining promises and exceeding expectations. Reputation compounds over time, attracting opportunities and partnerships. Entrepreneurs who prioritize short-term gains at the expense of trust often struggle later. AI amplifies both strengths and weaknesses, making reputation management more important than ever. Strong brands withstand competition because customers choose familiarity and reliability. Long-term operators invest in credibility as a core asset.

Financial resilience forms another cornerstone of the long-term playbook. Entrepreneurs must manage cash flow carefully, especially during periods of rapid change. AI tools assist with forecasting, budgeting, and identifying inefficiencies. Operators maintain reserves that allow strategic decisions rather than reactive ones. Financial discipline enables investment in new opportunities without compromising stability. Long-term profitability requires balancing reinvestment with sustainability. Entrepreneurs should avoid overexpansion driven by temporary success. AI provides visibility into trends that support informed financial planning. Stability creates freedom to innovate confidently. Financial resilience ensures survival through inevitable market shifts.

Leadership evolves as businesses mature, even for solo entrepreneurs. Operators must lead themselves with discipline while eventually guiding teams or collaborators. AI supports delegation by standardizing workflows and maintaining consistency. Leadership includes setting clear expectations and fostering a culture of continuous improvement. Entrepreneurs who develop leadership skills scale more effectively. Communication, decision-making, and accountability become increasingly important. AI handles operational tasks, but vision remains a human responsibility. Strong leadership ensures that growth aligns with long-term goals. Operators think beyond immediate profits toward sustainable impact. Leadership transforms businesses from projects into enduring organizations.

The AI Operator's Long-Term Playbook ultimately centers on adaptability anchored in strong principles. Tools will continue evolving, competition will increase, and market dynamics will shift unexpectedly. Entrepreneurs who rely solely on technology will struggle when the landscape changes. Those who build systems, cultivate relationships, and maintain discipline will thrive regardless of specific tools. AI becomes a constant ally when guided by clear strategy and intentional execution. Long-term profitability comes from combining innovation with stability. Operators view change not as a threat but as an opportunity to refine systems. Everyday entrepreneurs who adopt this mindset position themselves for enduring success. The future belongs to those who remain flexible without losing focus. When strategy, learning, and integrity guide decisions, AI becomes more than a tool—it becomes a long-term multiplier that sustains profitability through every stage of evolution.

AFTERWORD

The world has changed, and it will never slow down again. Artificial intelligence is not simply another tool added to the entrepreneur's toolbox; it is a defining shift in how ideas become income, how effort becomes leverage, and how ordinary people build extraordinary outcomes. Throughout this playbook, you have seen that success does not belong only to the largest companies or the most funded innovators. It belongs to the everyday entrepreneur willing to think clearly, act consistently, and build systems that multiply value. The tools are powerful, but they are not the hero of the story. You are the operator behind the system, the strategist behind the workflow, and the visionary behind the outcome. AI amplifies direction, but only you can choose the destination.

The future will reward those who move with intention rather than hesitation. While many will be distracted by endless features and constant innovation, the disciplined entrepreneur will focus on principles that endure: clarity, consistency, service, and execution. Income grows when systems replace chaos, when value replaces noise, and when trust becomes the foundation of every offer. You do not need to know everything to begin, and you do not need perfection to move forward. Progress belongs to those who build, test, refine, and keep moving. Every workflow you design, every product you launch, and every message you share becomes part of a larger engine working quietly on your behalf.

This is your moment to step fully into the role of operator, creator, and builder. The opportunity is not reserved for a select few; it is available to those willing to act with courage and discipline. Let others chase trends while you build systems. Let others wait for certainty while you create momentum. The playbook is now in your hands, and the next chapter is written by your decisions. Build wisely, serve deeply, and let intelligent leverage turn your daily effort into lasting impact and income.

ALSO BY DESHAWN PRICE

Toxic Amnesia: When Survival Becomes Self-Destruction

Toxic Strength: When Survival Looks Strong but Feels Empty

Toxic Control: When Fear Disguises Itself as Safety

Toxic Validation: When Approval Replaces Identity

Toxic Loyalty: When Faithfulness Becomes Self-Betrayal

Toxic Forgiveness -: When Grace Is Given Without Boundaries

Toxic Hope: When Waiting Turns Into Wasting Away

The Monetized Viral Machine: How to Build Posts That Pay

The Story-Selling Blueprint: Influence Hearts, Not Just Feeds

Victory Protocol: Strategic Habits That Produce Daily Wins

Your First Million: The Practical Path from Broke to Breakthrough

Millionaire Starting Now — The Fast Track to Seven Figures

The First Million Blueprint — Build Wealth with Precision

www.ingramcontent.com/pod-product-compliance
Lightning Source LLC
LaVergne TN
LVHW101617210926
848480LV00009B/705